First published in Great Britain in 1996 by Brockhampton Press, a member of the Hodder Headline Group, 20 Bloomsbury Street, London WC1B 3QA.

This series of little gift books was made by Frances Banfield, Kate Brown, Laurel Clark, Penny Clarke, Clive Collins, Melanie Cumming, Nick Diggory, Deborah Gill, David Goodman, Douglas Hall, Maureen Hill, Nick Hutchison, John Hybert, Kate Hybert, Douglas Ingram, Simon London, Patrick McCreeth, Morse Modaberi, Tara Neill, Anne Newman, Grant Oliver, Michelle Rogers, Nigel Soper, Karen Sullivan and Nick Wells.

ISBN 1 86019 446 X
A copy of the CIP data is available from the British Library upon request.

Produced for Brockhampton Press by Flame Tree Publishing, a part of The Foundry Creative Media Company Limited, The Long House, Antrobus Road, Chiswick W4 5HY.

Printed and bound in Italy by L.E.G.O. Spa.

# Just For You
# GRANDMA

### Illustrated by

*Douglas Hall*

A.R.C.A.

Selected by Anne Rose

BROCKHAMPTON PRESS

Mothers of our mother,
Foremothers strong,
Guide our hands in yours,
Remind us how
To kindle the hearth.

Celtic blessing

---

A grandmother always has time for you when the
rest of the world is busy.

Anonymous

---

Do not go gentle into that good night,
Old age should burn and rave at close of day;
Rage, rage against the dying of the light.

Dylan Thomas

My Grandmother said, 'Now isn't it queer,
That boys must whistle and girls must sing?
But that's how 'tis!' — I heard her say —
'The same tomorrow as yesterday.'
Traditional

A kindly gentleman encountered a four-year-old
standing on the street corner in deep perplexity.
'I want to run away,' the tot confided.
'Oh,' said the gentleman understandingly, 'why
don't you?'
'Well,' said the youngster, 'I'm not allowed to
cross the street.'
Anonymous

Married women, whatever their age, used to wear caps. Nowadays grandmothers kick up their heels in night-clubs ...

C. Webb-Johnson

Some grannies can watch TV while they sleep.
Some grannies have whiskers.
Some very special grannies can even take their teeth out.

Anonymous

God thought of all the lovely things
            She'd do to make life fun,
         and she created a Grandma
            To be loved by everyone

Anonymous

You see as the years roll on, we Grandmas need a Food that is easily digested and enjoyable at all times. We find Benger's a complete Food, fully nourishing and very delicious.

Benger's advertisement, 1930

Grandma was the heart of the family.
Her love and support were total and unconditional.
Marcy de Marée

She is foremost that I would hear praised.
  W.B. Yeats

It may be that we are all younger for our years than our grandmothers were, although I have a feeling that, whatever our grandmothers were, our great-grandmothers were minxes.

*Good Housekeeping*, 1930

Give me a good digestion, Lord,
And also something to digest.
  Prayer from Chester Cathedral

A secret is either not worth keeping or too good to keep.

Anonymous

We had an understanding, Grandma and I. She didn't treat me like a child and I didn't treat her like a mother.

Irma Bombeck

The pairing of young and old creates an openness not always found in adult relationships.

Suzanne Larronde

My grandma likes me being good.

Georgie, 4

Oh dear granny, we love you so
It's such a shame you have to go.
Come back soon!
Colin Hawkins, *The Granny Book*

'Dad, what are ancestors?'
'Well, my boy, I'm one of your
ancestors. Your grandfather is another.'
'Then, why do people brag about them?'
Old musical hall joke

The old are the precious gem in the centre of the household.

Chinese proverb

Judging by the world's press I am the only grandmother in the world.

Marlene Dietrich

Among the gloomy recollections of my life in bondage came tender memories of that good grandmother, like a few fleecy clouds floating over a dark and troubled sea.

Harriet Jacobs (Linda Brent), *The Good Grandmother*

Acqaintance; companion;
Once dear brilliant woman.
W. B. Yeats

---

A child of our grandmother Eve, a female;
Or, for thy more sweet understanding, a woman.
William Shakespeare, *Love's Labour's Lost*

---

A home without a grandmother is like an egg
without salt ...
Florence King, *Reflections in a Jaundiced Eye*

---

My grandmother was the wonder of my life for a
long while.
Mavis Nicholson

Two old-timers were discussing a mutual
friend. Said one, 'Poor old John seems to
be living in the past.'
'And why not?' replied the other.
'It's much cheaper.'
Anonymous

A man may not marry his Grandmother.
*The Book of Common Prayer*

It is as grandmothers that our mothers come into
the fullness of their grace.
Christopher Morley, *Mince Pie*

My grandmothers are
full of memories ...
My grandmothers were strong
Why am I not as they?

Margaret Walker (Alexander), *Lineage*

Every child should have a grandma as a strong
buttress against the world.

Anonymous

**G**race and thoughtfulness shine through
**R**adiantly in all you do.
**A**cclaimed for the advice you share,
**N**o one gives such love and care.
**D**early loved you'll always be,
**M**aker of sweet memories
**A**dmired by all your family.

Anonymous

For the pleasures that come from the world
bear in them sorrows to come. They come
and they go, they are transient: not in them
do the wise find joy.
Bhagavad-Gita

One of my grammas has died.
She was my best gran.
Jonathan, 6

Grandmothers have the time they never had as
mothers — time to tell stories, time to bear secrets,
time for cuddles.
Dr M. de Vries

Grandmother can be relied upon to
protect us from our mums and dads
when they are angry.

Anonymous

Then at last the waiting was over.
Mummy was going to the hospital to
have the baby. I didn't want her to go,
but I had Granny to look after me.

Catherine Anholt, *Aren't You Lucky!*

So many things we love are you, I can't
seem to explain except by little things,
but flowers and beautiful handmade
things — small stitches. So much of our
reading and thinking, so many sweet
customs and so much of our ... well
religion. It is all you. I hadn't realized
it before. This is so vague but do you see
a little, dear Grandma?

I want to thank you.

Anne Morrow Lindbergh, *Bring Me a Unicorn*

When a man surrenders all desires that come to the heart and by the grace of God finds the joy of God, then his soul has indeed found peace.

Bhagavad-Gita

The little boy started to cry after a large and friendly dog bounded up to him and licked his hands and face.

'What is it?' asked his mother. 'Did he bite you?'

'No,' sobbed the child, 'but he tasted me!'

Traditional joke

28

If nothing is going well, call your grandmother.
Italian proverb

Her manner of storytelling evoked tenderness and
mystery as she put her face close to mine and fixed
me with her big believing eyes. Thus was the
strength that was developing in me directly
infused from her.
Maxim Gorky

Once upon a time in a small village there was a little girl who was loved by everyone. Her grandmother was very fond of the child and on her birthday she brought her a present. It was a pretty red cape with a hood.
'Oh, Grandma, thank you!' said the girl. She liked it very much ...
*Little Red Riding Hood*

Granny's wants are simple
What she needs is you
To find her bag, her specs, her mag
And tune in to Radio 2.
Colin Hawkins, *The Granny Book*

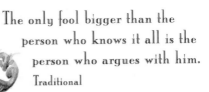

The only fool bigger than the
person who knows it all is the
person who argues with him.

Traditional

Brother (after quarrel):
'Sis, I'll meet you halfway.'
Sister: 'How?'
Brother: 'I'll admit I'm wrong,
if you admit I'm right.'

American joke

Wrinkles are hereditary. Parents get them from
their children.

Anonymous

The history of our grandparents is
remembered not with rose
petals, but in the laughter
and tears of their children
and their children's children.
It is not in us that the lives of grandparents
have gone. It is in us that their history
becomes a future.
Charles and Ann Morse,
*Let This Be a Day for
Grandparents*

God could not be every-
where so therefore he
made mothers.
Music hall joke

I like my grandmother because she is really nice
to me and lets me play with my friends.

Sophie, 7

---

If I'd known I was going to live so long I would
have taken better care of myself.

Anonymous

---

With mirth and laughter let old wrinkles come.

William Shakespeare

---

The great thing about getting older is that you
don't lose all the other ages you've been.

Anonymous

My grandmother sent me a new-fashioned
three-cornered cambric country cut
handkerchief. Not an old-fashioned
three-cornered cambric
country cut handkerchief, but a
new-fashioned three-cornered
cambric country cut handkerchief.
Traditional

My grandma is kind.
Mathew, 4

❖

... while I was a child her great affection for me,
and her intense care for my welfare, made me love
her and gave me that feeling of safety that
children need ... Her fearlessness, her public spirit,
her contempt for convention, and her indifference
to the opinion of the majority have always seemed
good to me and have impressed themselves upon
me as worthy of imitation.
Bertrand Russell

❖

The mother's heart is the child's schoolroom.
Henry Ward Beecher

You can't change the music of your soul.
Katharine Hepburn

Only two groups of people
fall for flattery — men
and women.
Traditional

I did not throw myself into the struggle for life: I threw my mother into it.
George Bernard Shaw

When you are old and grey and full of sleep,
And nodding by the fire, take down this book,
And slowly read, and dream of the soft look
Your eyes had once, and of the shadows deep.
W. B. Yeats

Five-year-old to his grandfather: 'Are you still growing?' 'Why do you ask, child?' inquired his grandpa. 'Well, the top of your head's coming through your hair!'

The creation of a thousand forests is in one acorn.
Ralph Waldo Emerson

Oh, yes, each man spoils the one he loves, and gratifies her wishes — the rich man showers her with gifts while the poor man does the dishes.

Anonymous

You can't spank Nana!

American proverb

To know how to grow old is the masterwork of wisdom, and one of the most difficult chapters in the great art of living.

Henri Frederic Amiel

And on that cheek and o'er the brow
So soft, so calm, yet eloquent,
The smiles that win the tints that glow
But tell of days in goodness spent,
A mind at peace with all below,
A heart whose love is innocent.

Lord Byron

What though youths gave
love and roses,
Age still leaves us friends,
family and wine ...

Thomas Moore

41

The happiest moments of my life have been
the few which I have passed at home in the
bosom of my family.

Thomas Jefferson

There is a chord in every heart that has a
sigh in it if touched aright.

Marie Louise de la Ramée

What closeness! Only the human animals
join so close; heart to heart ... see how that set
us and it apart ...

Susan Trott

The human heart, at whatever age, opens
only to the heart that opens in return.
Maria Edgeworth

Hearts live by being wounded.
Oscar Wilde

She took to children like a duck to water ...
years later ... she said she'd never, not until
she picked us up and cuddled us that very
first morning, known what men were for.
Angela Carter, *Wise Children*

You built no great cathedrals
That centuries applaud
But with a grace exquisite
Your life cathedralled God

Thomas Fessenden

Train your child in the way in which you know
you should have gone yourself.

C. H. Spurgeon

Let love and faithfulness never leave you; bind
them around your neck, write them on the tablet
of your heart.

*Proverbs* III:3

Grandma dear
Please don't tease
And may I have
The cookies please
American proverb

Where parents do too much for
their children, the children will not
do much for themselves.
Elbert Hubbard

45

The highest pinnacle of the spiritual life is not joy
in unbroken sunshine but absolute and
undoubting trust in the love of God.
A.W. Thorold

A mother has, perhaps, the hardest earthly lot;
and yet no mother worthy of the name ever gave
herself thoroughly to her child who did not feel
that, after all, she reaped what she had sown.
Henry Ward Beecher

Happy is the man that hath his
quiver full of them ...
*Psalms* 127:5

The family tree is worth bragging about if it
has consistently produced good timber,
and not just nuts.
Glen Wheeler

What is hard to endure is sweet to recall.
Bernard Shaw

How many loved your moments of glad grace.
W. B. Yeats

You are never so high as when you are on your
knees.
Jean Hodges

All that I am or hope to be,
I owe to my mother.
Abraham Lincoln

What sunshine is to flowers,
smiles are to humanity. They are
but trifles, to be sure, but,
scattered along life's pathways,
the good they do is
inconceivable.
Joseph Addison

48

Worry is like a rocking chair: It gives you
something to do, but it doesn't get you anywhere.
Anonymous

A man's work is from sun to sun, but a mother's
work is never done.
Anonymous

John: 'I'm glad you named me John.'
Mother: 'Why?'
John: 'Because that's what all the kids
at school call me.'
Anonymous

I remember my mother's prayers and they have
always followed me. They have clung to me
all my life.
Abraham Lincoln

A problem not worth praying about isn't worth
worrying about.
Glen Wheeler

She lullabyed us, she fed us. She was our air-raid
shelter; she was our entertainment;
she was our breast.
Angela Carter, *Wise Children*

Love is space and time made directly
perceptible to the heart.
Marcel Proust

O fairest flower no sooner blown but blasted,
Soft silken primrose fading timelessly,
Summers' chief honour if thou hadst outlasted
Bleak winter's force that made thy blossom dry;
For he being amorous on that lovely day
That did thy check en vermeil, thought to kiss
But killed alas, and then bewailed his
fatal bliss.
John Milton

I don't know who my grandfather was; I am much more concerned to know what his grandson will be.

Abraham Lincoln

I walked a mile with pleasure
She chattered all the way
But left me none the wiser
For all she had to say.

I walked a mile with sorrow
And ne'er a word said she
But oh the things I learned from her
When sorrow walked with me.

Robert Browning Hamilton

I was always told to respect my elders
It's just getting harder and harder to find one.
Traditional joke

※

The seven ages of women are: baby, infant, miss,
young woman, young woman, young woman,
young woman.

Anonymous

※

I've found the secret of youth — I
lie about my age.
Bob Hope

※

A mother is a mother still, the
holiest thing alive.
Samuel Taylor Coleridge

54

Daisies smell-less, yet most quaint,
And sweet thyme true,
Primrose, first-born child of Venus
Merry spring-time's harbinger.

The cowslip is a country wench,
the violet is a nun;
But I will woo the dainty rose,
The queen of everyone.
Traditional country rhyme

A lady with her daughter
or her nieces,
shine like a guinea and
seven-shilling pieces.
Lord Byron

In the heavens above
The angels, whispering to one another,
Can find, amid their burning terms of love,
None so devotional as that of 'Mother'.

Edgar Allen Poe

Who ran to help me when I fell;
And would some pretty story tell,
Or kiss the place to make it well?
My mother.

Ann Taylor

Mother is the name for God in the lips and hearts
of little children.

William Makepeace Thackeray

Nan, tonight you
wrapped me in the
warmth of your
memories and
your wisdom.
Tomorrow I will
see the world with
new eyes.
Kitty Browne

Thou, while thy babes around thee cling,
Shalt show us how divine a thing
A woman may be made.
William Wordsworth

Children are natural mimics; they act like their parents in spite of every attempt to teach them good manners.

Anonymous

'I'm not going to school anymore,' announced the youngster. 'It's a complete waste of time. I can't read and I can't write, and they won't let me talk.'

Playground joke

Perfection is attained by slow degrees; she requires the hand of time.

Voltaire

In all true love there is the love of the infinite in the person or thing we love.

Bhagavad-Gita

There is only one pretty child in the world, and every mother has it.

Traditional

The happy family is but an earlier heaven.

Anonymous

Our love was pure
As the snow on the mountains:
White as a moon
Between the clouds —
They're telling me
Your thoughts are double;
That's why I've come to break it off.
A cup of wine.
Tomorrow we'll part
Beside the canal.
Walking about, beside the canal:
Where it's branches divide
East and West.
Alas and Alas.
So must a girl
Cry when she's married,
If she find not a man of single heart,
Who will not leave her
Till her hair is white.
Cho Wen, *Chün*

# Acknowledgements:

The Publishers wish to thank everyone who gave permission to reproduce the quotes in this book. Every effort has been made to contact the copyright holders, but in the event that an oversight has occurred, the publishers would be delighted to rectify any omissions in future editions of this book.  Children's quotes printed courtesy of Herne Hill School, Hannah Rough and Kingfisher County Primary School; *Let This Be a Day for Grandparents*, Charles and Anne Morse, reprinted courtesy of St Mary's Press; *The Granny Book*, Colin Hawkins, reprinted courtesy of HarperCollins; Dylan Thomas, reprinted courtesy of the author's estate; *Collected Poems*, W. B. Yeats, reprinted courtesy of Macmillan Publishing Co. Inc., and A.P. Watt Ltd, London; *Mince Pie*, Christopher Morley, J. P. Lippincott-Raven and HarperCollins, New York; *Wise Children*, Angela Carter, Vintage, a division of Random House; 'The Cupboard', Walter de la Mare, from *The Complete Poems of Walter de la Mare*, 1969, reprinted courtesy of the Literary Trustees of Walter de la Mare and The Society of Authors.